Egypt

by Shirley W. Gray

Content Adviser: Professor Sherry L. Field,
Department of Social Science Education, College of Education,
The University of Georgia

Reading Adviser: Dr. Linda D. Labbo,
Department of Reading Education, College of Education,
The University of Georgia

 COMPASS POINT BOOKS

Minneapolis, Minnesota

FIRST REPORTS

Compass Point Books
3722 West 50th Street, #115
Minneapolis, MN 55410

Visit Compass Point Books on the Internet at *www.compasspointbooks.com* or e-mail your request to *custserv@compasspointbooks.com*.

Cover: Pyramid of Chefren in fog with the Great Sphinx below, Giza Plateau, Egypt

Photographs ©: Tom Till, cover; Jeff Greenberg/Visuals Unlimited, 4; John Elk III, 5, 6, 8, 9, 19, 20, 22, 25, 28, 36–37, 39; DigitalStock, 10, 13, 15, 41; Hulton Getty/Archive Photos, 11, 14; C. P. George/Visuals Unlimited, 12; TRIP/J. Pilkington, 16; McCutcheon/Visuals Unlimited, 17, 18; Joe McDonald/ Visuals Unlimited, 21; Jason Laure, 23, 24, 27; TRIP/H. Rogers, 26; Inga Spence/Tom Stack and Associates, 30; Inga Spence/Visuals Unlimited, 31; TRIP/A. Tovy, 33; TRIP/Mark Rogers, 34; TRIP/D. Saunders, 35, 40; Cheryl A. Ertelt, 38; Unicorn Stock Photos/H. H. Thomas III, 42–43; Norman Owen Tomalin/Bruce Coleman, Inc., 45.

Editors: E. Russell Primm, Emily J. Dolbear, and Deb O. Unferth
Photo Researcher: Svetlana Zhurkina
Photo Selector: Catherine Neitge
Designer: Bradfordesign, Inc.

Library of Congress Cataloging-in-Publication Data
Gray, Shirley W.
  Egypt / by Shirley W. Gray.
    p. cm. — (First reports)
  Includes bibliographical references and index.
  ISBN 0-7565-0126-1 (lib. bdg.)
  1. Egypt—Juvenile literature. [1. Egypt.] I. Title. II. Series.
  DT49 .G73 2001
  962—dc21
                                               2001001454

Table of Contents

Marhaba!

"*Marhaba!* Welcome!" You might hear this greeting if you visit Egypt. Visitors often arrive in the city of Cairo. It is the capital of Egypt.

▲ *Egyptian students learn about their country's history during a museum field trip.*

Egypt is also called the Arab Republic of Egypt. It is located on two continents. A continent is one of the seven great landmasses on Earth.

Most of Egypt is in northeast Africa. A small part of Egypt lies in southwest Asia.

▲ *Cairo is the capital of Egypt.*

▲ *The city of Dahab is on the Red Sea.*

Egypt touches three countries—Israel, Sudan, and Libya. A narrow part of Egypt separates the Mediterranean Sea from the Red Sea and the Indian Ocean. Years ago, people wanted to sail from one sea to another. This narrow piece of land blocked the way.

In the late 1800s, the French and the Egyptians cut a waterway through the land. This waterway is called the Suez Canal. Ships use the Suez Canal to get to Asia or east Africa.

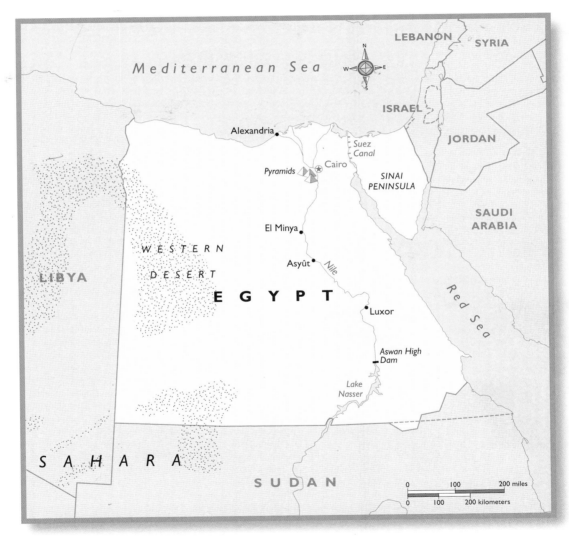

▲ Map of Egypt

The Land of the Sun

What would it be like if it never rained? The sky would be blue every day. You might never see a rain cloud. It is like that in Egypt. Every day the sun shines there. It almost never rains!

▲ *The sky is blue over Alexandria, Egypt's main port city.*

Egypt is a large country. It covers 386,662 square miles (1,001,455 square kilometers). It is much larger than the state of Texas, for example.

Almost all of Egypt is desert. A desert is a dry area with little water. During the day, the temperatures soar to more than 100° Fahrenheit (38° Celsius). At night, the temperatures fall quickly. The desert is very cold at night.

▲ *Most of Egypt is desert.*

▲ *The Sahara Desert*

The Sahara is the largest desert in the world. Part of the Sahara lies in western Egypt. Some places in the Sahara get no rain for years. Other places get a few inches of rain each year.

The Sahara gets little rain, but it does have storms—sandstorms. Each year, a strong wind blows for almost two months! The blowing sand forms huge hills called sand dunes.

Ancient Egypt

People have lived in Egypt for thousands of years. The early Egyptians were very skilled. They studied the stars and the sky. This study is called astronomy. They also made the first calendars.

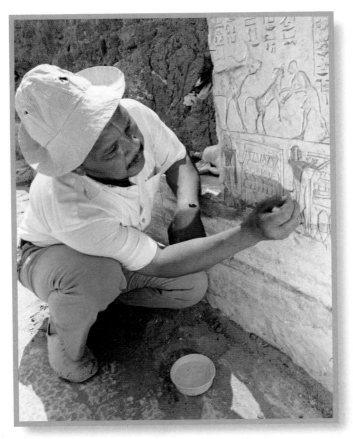

▲ *An Egyptian expert works on a 3,200-year-old building in Cairo.*

The ancient Egyptians made paper from a grass called papyrus. They drew pictures on the paper. The pictures told stories about the lives of the Egyptians and their gods. This kind of writing is called **hieroglyphics**.

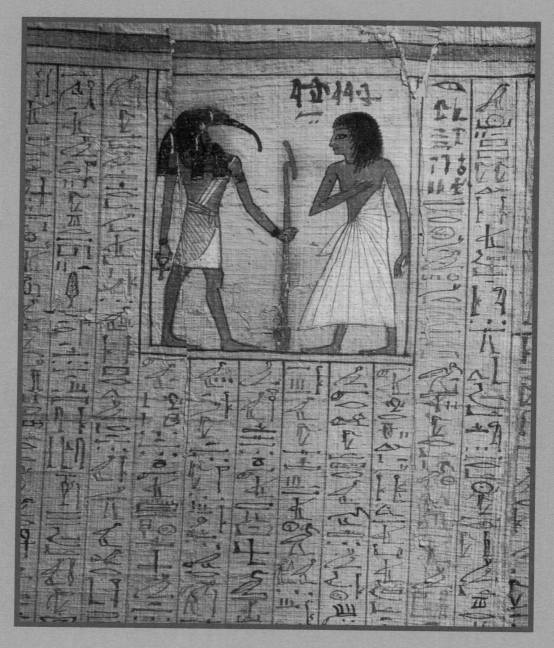

▲ *Egyptian hieroglyphics*

▲ *The Temple of Ramses*

Kings ruled ancient Egypt. These kings were called **pharaohs**. Some people believed the pharaohs were gods.

The pharaohs lived in palaces. Some of their furniture and clothing was covered in gold. Slaves built huge temples for them.

The Egyptians believed that after people died, they came to life again in another world. They believed animals came to life again too.

When someone died, the Egyptians wrapped the body in layers of cloth. This helped preserve the body for the next life. This wrapped body is called a **mummy**.

▲ *More than 100 mummies were discovered in the Western Desert in 1999.*

▲ *The Sphinx and the Great Pyramid of Giza*

The Egyptians built **pyramids**. The pyramids are big **tombs.** They put the mummies of pharaohs and queens inside.

▲ *The death mask of Tutankhamen*

The Egyptians also put tables, chairs, and food in the pyramids. They believed the pharaohs would need these things in the next life.

Egyptian workers dug tombs into cliffs on the Nile River. They made a tomb for a young king named Tutankhamen. This tomb is famous.

Thousands of people visit Egypt each year to see Tutankhamen's tomb and the pyramids. Visitors want to learn about the ancient Egyptians.

The Great Nile River

The Nile is the only river in Egypt. It is also the longest river on Earth.

The Nile starts as a tiny stream in the middle of Africa. It runs all the way through Egypt. Near the Mediterranean Sea, it branches into many small rivers and streams.

▲ *A farming area along the Nile between Luxor and Esna*

Most Egyptians live in cities or on small farms along the Nile. Every spring, the Nile River floods. These floods bring water and rich soil to the farms.

The ancient Egyptians did not know what made the Nile flood. They treated the river as a god. They threw gifts into the water hoping to make the god of the river happy.

▲ *A fisherman pulls a net from the Nile River near Edfu.*

▲ *Wheat and sugarcane are grown along the Nile.*

All year long, people use water from the Nile River. Egyptians built dams to hold the water back.

In southern Egypt, the Aswan High Dam stretches across the Nile. This dam holds water in Lake Nasser.

▲ *Lake Nasser*

Farmers take water from Lake Nasser through pipes or ditches. Then they can **irrigate** their fields. Today, farmers can grow crops even when there is no rain.

Many kinds of animals live near the Nile. The hippopotamus and the crocodile love to relax in the Nile. They can stay there all day because their eyes and nostrils are on top of their head. Just the top of their heads show above the water!

▲ *Crocodiles live in the Nile River.*

Life in Egypt Today

▲ Modern cars and wooden carts are common in Cairo.

On their way to school in Cairo, children pass buildings that are hundreds of years old. Some parents drive new cars from the United States or Europe. Other people travel to work by donkey or camel. They ride through the city streets! In Egypt, the old and the new are side by side.

The prime minister is the head of the government in Egypt. Egyptians who are eighteen years old or older can vote in elections.

By law, every child in Egypt must go to school. Sadly, this law is not enforced. Many children and adults in Egypt cannot read or write.

▲ *Egyptian schoolchildren*

▲ *Traditional Egyptian flat bread is ready for sale.*

Just like children in the United States, children in Egypt enjoy fast food. An Egyptian child might eat a *gyro* instead of a hamburger. This is a sandwich made with pita bread. It is filled with sliced lamb and served with a yogurt sauce.

At home, Egyptian families eat fresh fruits and vegetables. They also eat bread called *aysh*.

Beans are often served with eggs for breakfast. They are also cooked with vegetables for lunch or dinner. Sometimes they are mashed, fried in a patty, and served on aysh.

▲ *Fresh vegetables are sold in the market.*

People and Religions in Egypt

The Bible tells many stories about ancient Egypt. During the Roman Empire, most Egyptians were Christians.

Years later, the Arab Muslims came to Egypt. They taught the faith of Islam.

Today, Islam is the official religion in Egypt. Only a small number of Egyptians are Coptic Christians.

▲ *The St. Catherine Monastery near Mount Sinai was started in 547.*

▲ *Muslim men pray.*

The Muslims call God *Allah*. They pray on their knees to Allah five times a day.

▲ *A Nubian house in Aswan*

The laws of Egypt are based on the Islamic religion. Islamic laws are very strict. Mostly, the people of Egypt obey the country's laws. There is little crime in Egypt.

The Muslims use the Islamic calendar. One of their months is called Ramadan. Muslims believe that long ago the prophet Muhammad gave them the Koran during this month. The Koran is the holy book of the Muslims.

During Ramadan, Muslims **fast**. They eat and drink only after the sun sets.

Another group of people in Egypt are called the Nubians. They live in southern Egypt. They are not Arabs.

For hundreds of years, the Nubians lived and fished along the Nile River. Then, in the 1960s, the waters from the Aswan Dam flooded their homes. The Nubians had to move farther north.

Life in the Farm Villages

Some families along the Nile River are farmers. In Egypt, farmers are called *fellahin*.

Farmers in Egypt grow crops and take care of their animals just as their parents and grandparents did. Cotton, wheat, and corn are common crops.

▲ *A farm family in Egypt*

▲ *A young boy herds sheep and goats.*

Everyone in the family has a job on the farm. Water buffalo or oxen help with the heavy work. The mother weaves cloth for clothing. She also bakes bread every day. The children help in the fields and take care of the animals.

Today, the farmers in Egypt have new farm machines. The Aswan High Dam provides electricity for them. Some farmers bring water to the fields with electric pumps.

There are also new roads. People drive to the market in cars and trucks.

▲ *The Aswan High Dam*

Home in the Desert

▲ *Bedouins live in the desert.*

For hundreds of years, a group of people called the Bedouins have lived in Egypt. In the winter, they move from place to place in the desert. In the dry summer, some Bedouins move to areas with more water.

Bedouins sleep in tents made of goat hair. They keep herds of goats and camels.

▲ *A Bedouin tent*

▲ *A young Bedouin girl*

Bedouins wear long robes made of cotton or wool. These clothes protect them from the sun and blowing sand.

Men and boys wear pants and caps with their robes. Women and girls wear long dresses with sleeves. Black veils often cover their faces.

Date palms grow at the Siwa Oasis.

Some Bedouins live in small villages near **oases**.
An oasis is a place in the desert where there is water
and plants grow.

Each day, Bedouin women and children get water

from wells in the oasis. The women fill large jugs with water. They carry them on their heads.

Date palms are plants that grow near oases. Their long roots grow deep into the ground to find water.

Animals in the Desert

Although the desert is dry and hot, many animals live there. Snakes, lizards, and scorpions hide in the sand and rocks.

Many of the snakes are poisonous. One poisonous snake is called the horned viper.

▲ The horned viper

▲ *The desert is home to many animals.*

Desert animals can live on very little water. When there is no water, they eat the leaves of desert plants. Most sleep during the day and are awake at night.

The Bedouins and others travel across the desert on camels. Camels can walk easily on sand and over rocks. They can travel for weeks with no food or water. They store water and fat in their humps.

▲ *A camel train travels through the desert.*

Visiting Egypt

Each year, people from around the world visit Egypt. They visit the big cities of Cairo and Alexandria. They also come to learn more about the people who built the pyramids.

▲ *The City of the Dead in Cairo is a group of Islamic cemeteries that goes back 1,200 years.*

If you visit Egypt, you will learn more about this special country. When you leave you may say, "*Shukran!* Thank you! I had a good time in Egypt!"

◀ *Camels near the Pyramid of Chefren*

Glossary

fast—to give up eating food for a short time

hieroglyphics—ancient Egyptian writing using pictures and symbols

irrigate—to supply water for crops

mummy—a dead body that has been preserved

oases—places in the desert where there is water and plants grow

pharoahs—kings of ancient Egypt

pyramids—burial places of pharaohs

tombs—graves, rooms, or buildings for holding dead bodies

Did You Know?

- Hieroglyphs were written right to left, left to right, in columns, and in lines.

- The study of Egypt is called Egyptology.

- Cats became pets in Egypt more than 4,000 years ago.

- The tomb of King Tutankhamen was discovered in Egypt's Valley of the Kings in 1922. It is considered the most important archeological find of the twentieth century.

At a Glance

Official name: Arab Republic of Egypt

Capital: Cairo

Official language: Arabic

National song: "Beladi" ("My Homeland")

Area: 386,662 square miles (1,001,455 square kilometers)

Highest point: Jabal Katrinah, 8,651 feet (2,639 meters)

Lowest point: Qattara Depression, –436 feet (–133 meters)

Population: 69,146,000 (2000 estimate)

Head of government: Prime minister

Money: Pound

Important Dates

639–642	Muslim armies conquer Egypt.
1517	Ottoman Empire attacks Egypt.
1798	Napoleon conquers Egypt.
1801	British and Ottoman troops force the French out of Egypt.
1869	The Suez Canal is completed.
1882	British troops occupy Egypt.
1914	Egypt becomes a protectorate of the United Kingdom.
1940–1942	Several World War II battles are fought in Egypt.
1953	Egypt becomes a republic.
1967	Egypt is defeated in a war against Israel.
1970	Anwar el-Sadat becomes president of Egypt.
1981	Sadat is murdered.
1990	Egypt helps defeat Iraq in the Gulf War.

Want to Know More?

At the Library

Jay, David. *Read about Ancient Egyptians*. Brookfield, Conn.:
    Millbrook Press, 2000

Pluckrose, Henry. *Egypt*. Danbury, Conn.: Franklin Watts, 1999.

Shuter, Jane. *The Ancient Egyptians*. Austin: Raintree/Steck-Vaughn,
    2000.

Stanley, Diane. *Cleopatra*. New York: William Morrow, 1994.

On the Web

Egypt Fun Guide

http://www.seaworld.org/Egypt/egypt.html

For games and fun facts about Egypt

Life in Ancient Egypt

http://www.clpgh.org/cmnh/exhibits/egypt/index.html

For an online exhibit of Egyptian artifacts

Through the Mail

The Institute of Egyptian Art and Archeology

3750 Norriswood Avenue

Communication and Fine Arts Building

Memphis, TN 38152

To learn about this organization's work

On the Road

The Metropolitan Museum of Art

1000 Fifth Avenue

New York, NY 10028

212/535-7710

To tour an amazing Egyptian exhibit

About the Author

Shirley W. Gray received her bachelor's degree in education from the University of Mississippi and her master's degree in technical writing from the University of Arkansas. She teaches writing and works as a scientific writer and editor. Shirley W. Gray lives with her husband and two sons in Little Rock, Arkansas.